**TRIUMPH HOUSE**
Poetry with a Purpose

# TODAY, TOMORROW AND FOREVER

Edited by

Kelly Deacon

First published in Great Britain in 1999 by
TRIUMPH HOUSE
Remus House,
Coltsfoot Drive,
Woodston,
Peterborough, PE2 9JX
Telephone (01733) 898102

HB ISBN 1 86161 534 5
SB ISBN 1 86161 539 6

# FOREWORD

Today, poetry has become a more recognisable form of expression and communication. Different styles are used by different authors; and from traditional to contemporary, all are included in this carefully and well thought out anthology.

Over 100 new and established writers featured in *Today, Tomorrow and Forever* share their thoughts, feelings and views with you, the reader.

With some of the best poetry emerging today, we assure you that the book is an exciting and inspiring joy to be read time and time again.

Kelly Deacon
Editor

# CONTENTS

# BEYOND TOMORROW

Who knows what may be tomorrow?
No one but God above
As a new Millennium dawns
Let us trust His merciful Love!

Tomorrow may be far too late
For souls who are in need
Someone longs for our help today,
We give but little heed.

Beyond a new Millennium
Two thousand ages on
Spirits of Hope and Peace endure
In Jesus, God's own Son.

Beyond hours of pain and sorrow
Each morning with the dawn
New light comes to humanity
Where hope hides so forlorn.

Beyond Earth's misty, cloudy day,
Beyond the coldest night,
Beyond the darkest shadows
A rainbow's gleaming bright.

Beyond our Saviour's promises
He is alone the Key
To kingdoms past and present, all
Tomorrow's yet to be.

Arise, gladly meet the new age
Put courage on and see,
How all the world is waiting, for
God's truth shall set us free.

*Joan Heybourn*

# PHONE CALL

Pick up the phone to chat to a friend
So much quicker than a letter to send
Dial a fortune telling number
To hear in advance and then left to wonder
Emergency, yes, Police, Ambulance or Fire
Or 192 if you need to enquire
Pestering salesmen can get on your wick
You can ring a telly quiz, but you have to be quick
Phone at a distance, far over seas
But it's not cheap, do remember this please
Sing Happy Birthday over the phone
Ring with a message if you're to be late home
Then maybe the doctor you would ring in the night
Only of course if you're in some sort of plight
The vets or a taxi or maybe a shop
Theatre or pictures there are quite a lot
Times of transport you may need to find out
A day off school or work, you'll report all about
Use for appointments and cancellations too
The phone can be a Godsend to you
Going on holiday you may book in advance
When there's a bargain you can't miss a chance
A piggy bank is handy to save for the bill
The more calls you make the more it will fill
For the talking clock dial one, two, three
This voice on the phone is as clear as can be
When you've been out 1471 you can ring
Then you could return your last call now that you're in
We are so lucky we have this device
If you haven't got one, get one, that's my advice.

*Hazel Bowman*

# THE POWER OF POETRY

Telephone, telegram, tell a friend,
A post card from holiday sent,
Smoke signals, semaphore, drums,
Flowers with loving intent.

Good old snail mail (that's postal delivery),
Or air or high tech e-mail;
Morse code or hieroglyphics,
Sign language, lip reading, braille.

Newspapers, radio, telly,
A pigeon or dove on the wing,
Walkie talkie or citizen's band,
Empty tins tied together with string.

From the earliest whistles and grunts
To the latest techno' advance,
We've used them all, but I think there's one,
Against which none stand a chance.

For effective communication,
Has relied since the dawning of time,
On the power of its delivery,
And there's nothing more striking than rhyme.

*P Sharratt*

# INNOCENT LOVE

Each step is vital,
In this critical situation.
Every footstep taking them further away from home,
Away from danger.

A momentous atmosphere,
With crucial decisions every second.
From behind they can hear screams,
Then a haunting silence.

Children cling to their mothers,
Undoubtedly victimised.
Put through this inhuman suffering,
At stake of eternal terror.

Witnessing their own people,
Being brutally slaughtered.
Gunshots echoing in the distance,
The war is at its worst.

People all around them,
Collapsing with hunger and exhaustion.
And like so many other thousands,
They're innocent.

But the families flee in silence,
Believing that someone will guide them to safety.
Carrying on out of faith,
And clinging to anything that's left of hope . . .

*Stephanie Reynolds  (12)*

# CONNECTIONS

The telephone is a great invention
To instantly speak to someone you know.
To have two-way talks, with good intentions
To help lift you up, when you're feeling low.
Throughout the World you can call up a friend
Speak to relations without long visits.
Communications on which we depend
You only have to key up some digits.
The picture telephone will soon be here
Then we will have to make sure we look good.
It will be nice to see loved ones so dear
To care about each other, like we should.
Photography is wonderful also
Seeing our ancestors before we go.

*D M L Ranson*

## HIDDENNESS

'Where do You hide Your presence?' they cry throughout the earth.
Alone within the heavens? A cosmos-cosmic birth.
Gathered from the earthly dust, bonded by Your loving trust.
Conceived and born without the womb, racing onward to the tomb.
The first age found You tending a new and frightened flock,
Today we sigh and motion toward the doomsday clock.
Where are You, now we need You? . . . No miracles perform.
The past on paper yellows . . . The lull before the storm.
Well and truly eaten, manna had its day.
All alone and beaten, victims of the fray.
Bring forth Your face and greet us, as You did before,
Walk with us and talk with us, and mind our step once more.
No more of Armageddon, no more apocalypse,
No approaching horsemen, forth from furthest tips.
We need You now, among us, to see us safely through.
You made us, Ecce homo! Now tell us, where are You?

*Shirley Sammout*

# THANK YOU

*(Dedicated to Stove King)*

Thank you for your kindness,
It really pulled me through.
The darkest times that shrouded,
Days I never knew.
You'll never know how grateful
To you I'll always be,
Allowing me to write my words
And set all feelings free.
You probably don't realise,
Completely unaware
That I was able to move on
Because you were there.
The thoughts I had inside my head
had to be revealed,
Talking never cured my pain
I needed more to heal.
My only other option
Was to write those words
To clear my head of pressure
I needed to be heard.
Not ever really knowing why,
Poured out my heart to you,
Sealed my thoughts and sent away,
At last I faced my truth.
Reflecting on events gone by
To how I feel today,
'Thank you' seems such small a word
For what I want to say.

*Caroline Josephine Sammout*

# VE DAY

See the queue come join it quick
miss it then we'll get some stick
from Mother who says 'Jump right in
wartime rations are running thin.'

Air raid sirens give no respite
from doleful wailing late at night
Hitler, it seems, is no night sleeper
sending bombers with their grim reaper.
Hoping to catch us as we doze
raining death to bring us woes.

Hurry to school with gas masks ready
dash to the shelter with nerves unsteady.
The all clear sounds, so out we all come
'Hooray, look what's happened, our school has gone.'

Give us your pans, we'll make some bullets
fill our back yards with pigs and pullets.
'Dig for Victory,' we hear their cry
as barrage balloons cover the sky.
What's that a dog fight, 'twixt Brit. and Hun?
We give a cheer as Jerry's shot down.
Not thinking of him his life cut short
in a child's mind it counts for nought.

Now we are older and wiser they say
so World Peace we pray for this VE Day.
Let us not glorify those days gone by
just remembering the good times with many a sigh.
How we all worked together sharing our fears
laughing and joking to banish our tears.

But remember the evils that Hitler has done
remember the young lives so quickly gone.
Their blood stained our earth, the marks are still there
their courage beholds us to take far more care.
To share with each other one common cause
With tolerance and patience there'll be no more wars.

*Joan A Knipe*

## GHOST

I am floating, I am glowing,
I am like a human being but I am a ghost.
People don't know how I feel.
Some can see me but I'm not real.
I float about behind your back,
I flap about, then I attack!
I make a noise like a wolf that howls,
I come out at night and sing to the owls.

*Lauren Sammout  (6)*

## COMPANIONS

They shared my life for nigh on thirty years . . .
Proud heads . . . bright eyes
And oh, so willing feet
That trod the lanes so eagerly
And I'd follow willingly
Each joyous day to greet.

I saw the seasons through their eyes . . .
Green fields of summer damp with morning dew
That would renew the spirit's winter sojourn
And bluebell glades . . .
Where squirrels played reborn in springtime's fervour . . .
An epilogue to icy flows that danced upon the river.

A flash of black . . . or brown
Was seen to crown the brow of distant hills . . .
And I was filled with pride
When just one call would bring them to my side.
Wet paws . . . sleek coats . . . pink tongues . . .
Oh, how I long for the generous love they gave!

Sophie . . . first born . . . but not meant to be alone . . .
For Lucy came to fill the place
And with such grace and laughter filled our home.
Emma's need to be the queen . . . and Susie's completeness
Ne'er came between Emma's battles royal with Cora bold,
Who ne'er could be left in the cold.

And then one day God gave us Max . . .
Abandoned . . . tiny . . . but with such grit
That he lived his life in the fastest lane
And his time on earth was swift.
Dear God . . . give them all a voice in Heaven
As I wait my turn to make it 'seven'!

*Jean Makin*

# MY BEST FRIEND

How does he know when it's time for a walk?
I swear I can see him smile
What tells him which way I've decided to go -
What takes him that one extra mile?

How can he tell to the minute, no less
When I think of opening a tin
And does he think I've forgotten the food
And even which cupboard it's in?

How does he know when I'm feeling low
And can he understand
How much he does for me in the way
He puts his paw in my hand?

And in his eyes, the wag of his tail,
Can anyone possibly know
That this faithful creature some label as 'dumb'
Really knows more than we'll ever know?

***Donald S Ferguson***

## SITTING PRETTY

The bow that I wear in my dishevelled hair,
I'm wearing to make your face smile,
I know I look cute, and that I'm a beaut,
For I'm brushed and I'm combed all the while.

I *can* cut up rough, but my owners' get tough,
For they make me do just as I'm told,
When I try to defy them, their stern looks belie them,
To them, I'm more precious than gold!

This Yorkie toy pup, can really play up,
I can twist them both round my small paw,
I know they both love me, place no one above me,
I can't ask for anything more.

I know you can't see but they've photographed me,
To send on a customised card,
To a birthday-girl friend, on its way it will wend
With greetings composed by 'the Bard'.

The Bard is my mum, I'm her very best chum,
As you will have gathered, no doubt,
The card is now done so we'll go for a run,
Well - a walk, for she's taking *me* out!

We live at the coast - when the card's in the post,
We'll make our way down to the sea
In which we shall paddle before we skedaddle,
Back home where we'll all have our tea.

***Doreen Jones***

## PANGOR

Lovely and sleek
Shiny and black
A feline of note
My friend of long standing
She purrs at my feet
Independent she is
And make no mistake
Those shiny green eyes
Say with a glance
I own you
You don't own me.
But when I sit on my chair
By a bright glowing fire
She hops on my lap.
As my hand strokes her fur
A paw put in my hand
Says it all without word
We are friends for all time.
A lovely black cat
And a happy bright me.
We go for a walk
Pangor and me
She is careful in steps
Lest dirt touches paws.
So with a soft little meow
She jumps up on my shoulder.
The value of her friendship
Is beyond silver or gold
In the world of today.

***Brigid O'Donnell***

# THE ADVENTURER

We once owned dogs, Barry and Shandy his brother.
Barry was obedient, loving and loyal
Shandy too, was loving, but, an absolute trial.
Every day, Barry was as good as gold
Shandy, however, was so naughty and bold.
He chewed almost everything in sight
And was always ready for a good play fight.
He disappeared at regular intervals,
'Sorry pals, but, adventure and destiny calls'
Mostly he came home on his own accord
Often, the police put him up, with bed and board.
We would fence him in and play ball games
But, he would still escape, in spite of our aims.
The muddiest most stagnant pool, would find him immersed
Or rolling lazily in cow pats, or something much worse!
We once collar-cuffed him to his brother
Hoping this would curtail our escapee lover.
The exercise backfired to our dismay
With loyal Barry being dragged away.
Hastily, we caught and retrieved the pair
The relief on Barry's face was extremely clear,
After all, once he had passed the puppy stage
He was content to act his age!
Not so Shandy, he never changed
He had just wanted the world re-arranged.
He happily grew old most disgracefully
And stayed true to form quite faithfully.
The old boy behaved as a pup, right up to the end
But, like his brother, remained this woman and man's best friend.

*Vivienne Doncaster*

# TV

How lovely it would be without TV.
The restful peace and quiet day by day
Would let the bird song steal upon the air,
The buzz of bees, the crickets in the hay.

No voices of presenters loud and shrill,
No films with gunshot ringing in our ears.
The silence would be balm to tired nerves,
A quietness not know for several years.

But, 'Isn't it the time for Emmerdale?'
'Oh, Mum, 'The Gladiators' is now due,'
'What's happened to the 'News at 10' this time?'
'The Philharmonia Concert's right on cue.'

The TV has become a part of life,
A few days quiet and we feel the loss.
We don't know what is happening in the world,
The television has become the boss.

We need the background sound to reassure,
We are in touch with what is going on.
We can join in the conversation too,
And criticise the programmes that have gone.

If we are ignorant of all the soaps,
And do not know why Sharon is not wed
Or whether Tiffany fell down the stairs
Or was pushed, as some of the neighbours said.

We cannot join in as our hair is set,
(The hairdresser is asked to referee).
The days of no TV have long since gone,
So we go home to honey and TV.

*Joyce M Turner*

## WHY?

Why we ask, why we pray, these are our questions of today.
But no one seems to know what to do
Bombs and gun smoke all around, making holes in the ground.
Boys so evil and sour within souls of mischief and of sin,
Why we ask, what's it for, we are in a 'Good Land' of mercy not war.
But somehow, out there, before us, some don't really care;
Pain and sorrow is what it's all about, even people stand and shout
Does no one listen to our plea to free us from this world
of sin and free our souls of misery.
To stop and hear laughter to even a cry of a child will do
But gun smoke bombs are all around, these seem the only sounds,
It's worse than when the war you'll hear them say,
we fought to free us for this day.
Now all seems at a loss no one knows whose friend or foe even you
will say my this is a sad tale of woe.
But head held high and fly the flag is the call all about,
Keep on smiling and good will prevail, overwhelm the evil
that's here today.

*Elizabeth A Wilkinson*

## MOBILE PHONES ARE GREAT

Mobile phones are great,
You can use them to ring your mates,
If you need picking up from somewhere,
And don't want to pay a bus fare,
Then use your phone,
(or you could loan)
And a relative will come.

You can carry them around
And they cost about seventy pounds,
They come big or small,
And you can use them to call,
From anywhere,
Without a card,
Plus they're so easy to use!

'Do you want to go to town?'
Is one of the questions asked,
Without a phone how would we ask?
No one would have a social life,
Or get to see a film,
So, thankyou, to Alexander Graham Bell.

*Jennifer Bull*

# TALK, TALK, TALK

Communication from the start,
Has always been a special art,
Semaphore with flags, dot dash for morse,
Pony express on a very fast horse.

Racing through time, communication gets faster,
Telephones used to be owned by the master,
Now everyone's got one, an everyday thing,
Even dial a number to hear someone sing.

Now creeping in to the twenty-first century,
Communication is just a computer entry,
You don't have to go out, you don't have to talk,
Switch on the computer, teach fingers to walk.

Where are we going, is this really better,
Not quite the same as writing a letter,
And what would happen if all this went wrong,
All that equipment would go for a song.

Verbal communication is going out of fashion,
Losing the contact, the dialogue, the passion,
Don't let technology take too high a place,
The best communication takes place face to face.

*Amanda Giddings*

## I'M A LONELY RABBIT

I sit all alone, all day in my hutch,
I don't think you care about me so much,
The only time you take any notice of me,
Is when you have friends around for tea.
Then you hold me, and pet me, and give me some grass,
Then back in my hutch, - I knew it wouldn't last.
When you first brought me home, away from the shop,
You'd rush back from school calling, 'Come on *Flip Flop*.'
That name it is stupid, fancy calling me that,
Didn't you know I was an Aristocrat.
When I was tiny, a white ball of fluff,
My ears long and silky, tail a white powder puff
You'd then take me out, stroke me, and squeeze me,
Wouldn't leave me alone even when I was sleepy,
You let me hop on the grass, watch me jump all around
You'd laugh at my antics, I had you spell-bound.
Now all that has changed, what have I done wrong?
Sometimes my hutch has a terrible pong,
When my straw needs changing, you do not do it
No, your Mum does that now moaning, she always knew it,
I hear your Dad shouting, 'And I'm telling you so,
If you don't feed that Rabbit it will just have to go.'
You do feed me occasionally, give me something to munch.
I'd rather have a cuddle than a carrot to crunch.
Oh well, I sit all alone, all day in the sun,
Now if I had a friend here, I could really have fun . . .

*Barbara Servis*

## My Only True Friend

I gently stroke her
Smooth coat of silk
As I pour her
Another saucer of milk.

For she is always there
When times are rough
My true companion
When things are tough.

For by my side
Is where she will always be
And no matter what I do
She will never judge me.

That is why she is
My only true friend
And I hope that this
Will never end.

I know that she loves me
As much as I love her
I know that she is content
When I hear her purr.

Her name is Ginger
With eyes so fair
Lying peacefully
Asleep on my chair.

*Ian Fowler*

## GOLDEN RAINBOWS

I always said 'I'd have no dog'
I'd have to walk in rain and jog
Then a friend, who knew I'd time to spare
Came to see if I would share
My life, with a dog who had no home
Who could keep me company when alone
So I promised to take just one look
I never knew that's all it took.
When she came to visit for a day
I never dreamed that she would stay
A little dog with golden hair
Who stole our hearts without a care
She filled our dreams and all our lives
This little dog was idolised
But time passed swifter than we knew
Her years with us were far too few
She paid the price for life's neglect
That all our care could not correct
Safe, secure, her gratefulness showed
How easily we love her, how hard to let go.
She passed through our lives, never destined to stay
Destiny brought her, then took her away
Over the rainbow, so I'm told
You can find a pot of gold
But its always my hope, that I'll find there
My little dog with golden hair.

*Carole Hartshorne*

# CAT

You prowl about
Like some proud lioness,
Lording it over your territory,
Terrorising the cats next door,
And any dogs
Who dare hove in sight.

You claim ownership
Of this family
And all its possessions,
Using us for your
Multifarious purposes
As of right.

You communicate your
Needs to us,
Asking to be fed,
Or let out,
Demanding attention at all hours
Of the day and night.

You are loved, spoilt,
Cosseted, cherished, adored
By us, your willing
Human slaves,
Oh cat, so perfectly
White.

*Monni Aldous*

## OUR DAY OUT

We went for a stroll in the country
just me with Rex by my side.
The scenery was very beautiful
across country far and wide.
The sky was baby-blue in colour
there wasn't a cloud to be seen.
The sun was shining brightly
everywhere looked nice and green.
In the field there was a farmer
reaping in the hay.
Preparing for the harvest
he'd be working there all day.

Then we passed two horse riders
they were looking pleased to be out.
Cattle in a field were grazing
lambs and sheep skipping about.
Then we came to a house
with children all happy at play.
Their parents sitting in the garden
enjoying the marvellous day.
Rex my dear old faithful
stopped and barked up at me.
Telling me it's time to go home
it was nearly time for his tea.

*Keena*

# CULL THE GULL

Soar, soar, soar like a gull,
twist in the wind skimming the sea,
climbing cumulus for a better view.

Preening feathers to waterproof
laying eggs on flat felt roofs,
dropping shells to break on through.

Picking bins to fill a belly
worm dance on the green valley lawn.
Laying eggs on the cliff's seashore.

Swooping on a rival male
to score and keep a mate - female.
Biting beak with serrated edge
sword fight to the bitter end.

To keep your lifetime companion friend,
until a voted savage cull.

*A J Lagadu*

## BECKY

I so adore my dog Becky,
who is eleven years old;
She gives me much joy ev'ry day,
and is lovely to behold.

A very happy female pet
is Becky, the beagle hound;
She loves her food, her walk, her bed,
and is nice to have around.

My dog Becky is very good,
and does love to wag her tail;
At my feet she is often stood,
and even waits for the mail.

She asks me for her lead each day,
eager to go for her walk;
She hears ev'ry word that I say,
and she also tries to talk.

The Vicar in his kindly way
so adored his faithful friend.
He took her out every day,
and he loved her to the end.

When he died, Becky adored me,
and went out with me instead;
So, at my side I let her be,
or asleep upon my bed.

But how shall I live without her?
Sad - I myself do not know;
I trust that the Lord will provide,
for I, indeed, love her so.

*Margaret R Bromham*

## SOULMATE

Love of my life
in silver fur.
He raises his eyes
in silent adoration.
Guardian of my life
in shades of grey.
He sleeps upon my bed
with gleeful jubilation.
And when his final
rest day comes,
'tis I, without his faithfulness
shall feel utter desolation.
My Monty, OES

*Ann Voaden*

# MY PET CROCODILE

Come and say hello
to my pet crocodile.
Its tears are wet
but insincere
as it moves
with organs of power.
It feeds on politicians,
tabloid newspaper editors
and agents that
take more than ten percent
and publishers who turn down my work.

As I walk down the street
with my pet crocodile,
people say 'Just look at those teeth!
It's the biggest crocodile
I have ever seen.
It must be Egyptian,
a serpent of the old Nile.
Did you see that?
It's just eaten a traffic warden
and that policeman's living in fear.
And now its eyes are on a publican
that charges too much for his beer.'

When I'm relaxing at home
with my pet crocodile,
it gives a look
that's hard to trust,
a look that seems to say
this house ain't big enough for both of us.

I'm sorry this poem must be cut short
as I disappear down my crocodile's throat.

**Ian Barton**

# PARROT ALARM

Brother's got a parrot keeps you awake,
starts up noisy every day-break.
Covers up the cage, to make it seem dark.
If it was a dog, I'm sure it would bark.
It's early morning, too soon to get up
I hear him call out for him to shut up.
Even though it's Sunday and we can lie in,
Parrot doesn't know or care
Still makes a din.

*F Williamson*

# A Cat Called 'Miss Marple'

I watched you die last night, my pet,
I felt such pain inside.
I tried hard to be brave for you
but tears I could not hide.
I've loved you all these years you see,
I willed you not to go.
I didn't want you leaving, because I loved you so.
Past memories flew before my eyes
of closeness and affection,
and with my heartfelt love
I gave you comfort and protection.
I looked into your golden eyes
the lustre was fast paling.
We both knew soon you'd have to go
your strength was slowly failing.
I smoothed your coat, I touched your face
and tears flowed down my cheek,
you couldn't purr nor utter,
because you were so weak.
Your dear sweet heart was slowing
whilst *my* heart was breaking so.
I kissed your head, spoke gentle words
I *begged* you not to go.
But from me you were taken
and I cradled you with sorrow,
not knowing, thinking *what* I'd do
without your love tomorrow.
Your soft warm body stilled
and I'm alone, without you now,
I know that life goes on
and I must live my life somehow.
One last sad kiss, a quiet goodbye
more tears of grief I see,

we wrap you tenderly in cloth
and lay you 'neath a tree,
to rest, to still be *near* us
as you start your last, long sleep.
But I never will forget you -
as your *memory* I will keep.

**Margaret Hanning**

## My Computer

I've got a borrowed computer
And a borrowed printer too.
You might say 'What is your problem?
Wish I was as lucky as you.'

But my computer and printer
do not agree you see.
They will not work together,
they are awkward as can be.

My computer said to me
'What is this thing you've got
connected up to my behind
plugged in my vacant slot?

No! I do not like this set-up
so this is what I say
in answer to your question.
No! It's not OK.

So if you want us to work together
just give me a disk to chew.
Then if I like what I read on it
I'll see what I can do!'

So I got the disk it wanted
and told it what to do for me.
Now the two of them work together
in perfect harmony.

*Iris Covell*

## WHEN WILL WE EVER LEARN?

'The war to end all other wars.'
Is what the people said,
In 1918 as they looked
Upon their *glorious* dead.

'This war should be the end to war!'
They said in '45,
As children lay upon the ground
Who should be still alive.

And yet with all succeeding years,
These so called *years of peace!*
The fighting never seems to stop
In fact, the wars increase.

One hundred years of war has failed,
It is for peace we yearn.
And yet the fighting still goes on
When will we ever learn?
When will we *ever* learn?

**David L Morgan**

## DRUMCREE PROTEST 1998

*(First published 'The Entertainer' - Issue IO - August 1998 under my previous pen name - Mary Jo West)*

Three murdered children in Northern Ireland.
Orange Order, Drumcree disorder.
Hillsborough Castle, RUC,
please will you try and keep matters in order?
Three young children murdered, how could this be?

Three bouquets left, a mark for three innocent young children.
The Quinn boys, relatives in tears,
The Orange Order, were they to blame?
I don't know, my person was not there.

I heard this news on my TV today,
Sunday the 12th July of this year.
I am in England, but I have friends in this place,
I fear for their safety, surely Peace should reign.

Easter, Bloody Sunday, surely Peace was to take place,
I felt the tears of people in this place across the sea.
I felt my heart cry. Peace, please let Peace reign?
I give my prayers to this family.

Three murdered children in Northern Ireland,
Please remember this, that children are innocent,
No matter what your hearts say, Roman Catholic or Protestant
Orangemen of this country, no matter who you are.

Think back to the beginning, were you not born an embryo being?
Not knowing what your life would be, you just came into history.
You keep a heartache alive, through generation and generation.
Please before you shoot, cause a bomb to explode,
Remember, what if these children had been your own?

History in the making, I am but a poet,
Thoughts of young children, no matter what country.
They find a way to my heart, and the words they just flow.
Please everyone, will you not say a prayer?
For children . . . everywhere.

*Josie Lawson*

# THE DIFFERENCE!

'Stay!'
I say to my dog.
She stays.
'Stay please?'
I say to my lover -
But she goes!

*Richard S W Neville*

# POLLY

My eyes search for pictures of you.
Silently I call your name
though I know you cannot come.
Yesterday you breathed my air
I watched and felt you near.
Today there is no you, you are no more.
Your face I cannot see.
You are not there to please me
I will always, always
remember when you were.
You will be stored in my memory bank
category five star, top drawer, always frequented.

*Jean Read*

## TINSPEAR - THE RACING PIGEON

'Tinspear' was the scourge of every pigeon cote in Bent
where all his wicked life he spent!
The Meyly bird ruled the roost, he frightened all the
other birds away, keeping his favoured hens at bay.
At every meal the black *peys and maze* were all soon
tucked away leaving nowt fort rest ut day!
The only way to get some rest, was to put Tinspear
up for sale in the local press!
Now half a crown wasn't much for such a magnificent
looking bird! So locals thought there must be a catch!
But many took a chance and bought him just the same,
much to their dismay.
For after just one day he'd have his wicked way
then fly back home again!
After many conquests and many more half crowns, he was
barred from every pigeon cote in Bent!
As a last resort Tinspear was kept under a bucket
with holes in it to keep the bird well aired, he was a
prisoner in his own back yard!
A terrible plight for Tinspear - biggest bird in Bent.
It would seem his days were numbered for this likeable
crafty bird, now easy prey for the local cats, as he
lay under the bucket on the ground.
Now Tinspear's chance of freedom came one very hot
summer's day. When the bucket was accidentally knocked away.
So once more the battered bird become the ruler of the skies.
Over the summer months Tinspear lived on the rooftops
and got easily fed, raiding every Pigeon cote taking
all their food and bread.
The winter months were upon us and food became so scarce
that Tinspear slowly began to starve.
The Pigeon cotes were all locked up, the frost made
his life so hard.

Tinspear's last chance to live was to return to the cote
from where he came, but he knew his life would never be the same.
As he tried to dive to safety, he dropped like a
falling stone, once more fate took a hand, when he
was lifted from the ground Tinspear was not expected
to live. When he heard a voice he knew.
'The pest won't see the winter through! Now at last
he's doomed.'
But Tinspear took his head from beneath his wing
then slowly puffed out his chest, opened one eye,
winked . . . then thought spring will be here soon!

**Ken Pendlebury**

## CHILD OF WAR

How well do I remember that awful wailing cry,
and Father saying 'There they go right across the sky.'
Then Mother bundled on our coats, and all with fleeting feet -
would rush head-long to uncle's shelter, where we all would meet.

How well do I remember, the night the bomber's came,
when Father couldn't quite get home and laid down in the lane.
I cried, and said I wanted Dad, but Mother said 'Be brave,
I'm sure the Jerries and their bombs won't make Dad afraid!'

How well do I remember, as a little girl of eight,
the day we had our gas-masks and found them quite a weight.
We then had a practice to get them on quick sharp,
but some of the children thought it quite a lark.

How well do I remember, the day the war was won.
The news came through the wireless and we knew Peace had come.
My, what rejoicing there was in every home;
People shouting, flags a-waving, no-one was alone.

The streets were soon decked out with tables,
a great big party had begun.
And we gave thanks to God our Father
for the victory that had been won!

*Olivia Wheatley*

# WILL YOU WRITE?

You can E-mail, fax or telephone
to an office or to someone's home.
Electronic communication is the thing
sat in front of a computer screen.
All very well for a business proposition
but not very nice in an informal situation.
And what I would like to know better
is whatever happened to the written letter?

*Melanie M Burgess*

# LIKE THE WALLS OF JERICHO

All through time as history shows, Dictators had held sway.
But come a time, some short, some long, they all have had their day.
Some systems start with mass appeal and fervent acclamation,
and end up with no liberty and, national strangulation.

The rationale is always thus 'It's for the State I act,
to give the common people power, and with them make a pact.
We are at one in all we seek, and power we will share,
but I need so much more than them, and that is only fair.'

It's said that power corrupts us all and that's an absolute.
So how much more will it corrupt, the egotist and brute?
The State becomes their deity, their all, their one excuse,
to treat all those within its bounds, with contempt and abuse.

So it was that freedom fled and *iron curtain* fell.
Transforming once free citizens, to denizens of hell.
Once proud nations now constrained, within an iron border.
With freedom and the world outside, erased by leaders' order.

But freedom is a state of mind and brooks no inhibitions,
ignoring rules and regimens and physical conditions.
And precedent and pressure prove a deadly combination,
destroying tyranny and hate and resurrecting nation.

Although there was no trumpet blast, no vibrant piercing sound.
The *Berlin wall* like Jericho's came tumbling to the ground.
The evil empire's just demise, long sought and much aspired.
Epitomised by crumbling wall and globally desired.

*Alfred J Smith*

## GOD'S TRUTH

If God for the whole truth, was yearning,
then which daily paper would He buy?
To which channel would He be turning
for the main news on which to rely?

And could He sift the wheat from the chaff,
or hear reason over all the din?
Would He be angry, or would He laugh
at the dissembling of men of spin?

What would He learn from those keen to teach
from whatever pulpit it may be?
Differing gospels do they all preach
but do they spread the word honestly?

Would He attend the management course,
where the corporate image holds sway?
Their own self-interest to endorse
and the truth sees not the light of day!

Today, voices are raised far and wide -
and yet, words have lost their true meaning;
Whilst, phrases are used, the truth to hide,
as new man goes strutting and preening!

If God, for the whole truth were to seek
would He not draw a blank on this Earth?
Where are His creatures honest and meek;
Where all words used are truly of worth?

*Roy Hammond*

# A VIEW

Who can now e'er foresee
a future for this thing TV?
The picture shows a square white wall,
the pictures on it not at all;
The amateur reigns just to fill a space,
the jewels and art have got no place.

'Old Music Hall must turn in its grave'
as with tawdry acts the show they pave;
It slides and stumbles like a fool,
perhaps forgetting the golden rule:
'Who needs you son?' come light of day,
If the answers none - you're on your way.

Think of pay as you view
or pay at the door,
Then how would be yearned
the Aunt Sally's of yore;
Art as before can cruelly turn
to parody jesters and fingers burn.

It all unfolds when we get to choose,
the winners win, and the losers lose;
Build bricks of straw and when it ends
find evening's late to make amends;
The time was there but it's going gone,
The party's over and moving on . . .

*Alistair McLean*

## SCARS OF YESTERDAY

Don't speak to me of war!
Don't preach to me of hate, my son!
Your unlearned eyes have never beheld
my learned hands at the gun!

I have seen you turn from my pipe on the hearth -
at my jacket faded and blue.
Your impatient smile at my placidity -
my routine's not new to you!
It is painful for me to look back on the war,
through the concave mists of fear and hate,
and tears. Oh! The tears for comrades lost!
The endurance tests of hell's gates!

'Twas like one fiendish dream!
Never-ending beat of a drum . . .

Victory's release!
My wife, my son
into my arms they came and I find
the *welcome home* sign -
forever printed like a blessing on my mind.

Home is my haven forever for me,
my England again I'll not leave.
I consider this modern world and I smile,
my endurance I cannot believe.

I'm content that this peace is for you my son,
though I know you would have fought too.
Perhaps one day you will realise
that my haven's a release from the blue.

*Angela B Vanes*

## THE MESSENGER KING

Such a face -
those kindly eyes,
a man of peace
to bear -
He travelled far
to spread his gift
with wisely words
of care -
Those expressive eyes
which spoke of love
that human-man
can find -
He stemmed the rage
of discontent
in many a warrior mind.
The desert nomads
held him dear
a pinnacle of respect -
For many years
they shared his hope
of the peace he would effect.
And this he did,
he took the strain
cajoled many a warrior heart -
For many years he travelled far
his message to impart.
And now he's gone
to a mystery realm -
yet may his treasured peace remain
forever in the hearts of man -
as we remember King Hussein.

*Mary Skelton*

## THE PHONE

One depends on the phone
just as ET needed to call home
to keep in touch
with the ones you miss so much
each blip
saves a trip
from each hall
one can arrange to have a ball.
Long distance communication
in anticipation
of time felt events
of time spent
of happy days that have been and went
echoes of distance places
as the world of progress races
the world is smaller
buildings taller
at the fingertips of the phone caller!

*Finnan Boyle*

# IT IS NOT RIGHT!

It is right that I feel sad looking at the flowers
below whose roots you lie dead.

It is right that I should cry thinking of you.

As the twilight sky presses heavily upon the dark green bows,
your piercing cry is absent. The same
herd of cows graze peacefully,
as if it did not matter that you are out of sight.
The same birds' chatter gets ready for sleep
their chirping subdued before the falling of night.

It is only right that my heart and soul should weep:
my arms missing your warm, silky body,
my ears listening for that contented purr
before going to sleep.
It is right that missing you, I weep.

But it is not right - I wish to cry out loud -
it is not right that one so loving, innocent and young
should be mortally hit and come to a sudden end.

It is not right, unless, unless . . .

Surely there must be a sound reason,
rather than a cruel fate's treason.
Surely a deeper meaning which I fail to comprehend.

*E R Vid*

## PURRING IN MY EARS

My cats are pleased
to see me up early.
Max and Lucy
they can have their breakfast
even if it is before
seven thirty.
I'm certainly thirsty
needing a cup of tea.
They purr profusely
how good to see them happy.
Spring is definitely
in the air
it's becoming bright
I'm all right
in spite of
a late night.
They awaken me in a
lovely way.
Where would I be
without them.
Bless them
little dears
purring in my ears!

*Kathryn Longley*

## NEVER TO BE FORGOTTEN
*(Anna)*

Wisps of straw, blown about in the breeze
pressures of life, carried with ease.
Relax on a summer's day
shared with a chestnut, coloured or bay.
Smell of leather and gleaming brass
(Now stand while tacked up, there's a good lass!)
Out on the ride, the world is yours
alone with your horse, a moment's pause.
Spectacular view makes you feel alive
these are the moments in which you thrive,
The thrill of the gallop, the wind in your hair,
no worries at all, without a care.
Home again, brush down and feed
looking after her every need.
She looks after you with love in her heart.
You know that you'll never part.

*J A McLennan*

## HEADMASTERS ARE INDIGESTIBLE

Now Matthew had a dragon. He kept it as a pet.
One day it had a tummy ache. He took it to the vet.
Those cats and dogs and rabbits, shrieked and swiftly vanished.
His pet surveyed the empty room and simply said 'I'm famished!'
The trembling vet said nervously 'I'll see what I can do.
But a brutish thing like this really should be in a zoo.'
The dragon didn't like his tone, in fact he said as much,
And added, were he better, he'd eat him for his lunch.
The vet applied the stethoscope, 'Breathe out, and in, and out.'
The dragon's breath was fetid, it knocked the poor man out.
Matthew pulled his pet outside and wiped away a tear,
Then he remembered that the friendly chemist's shop was near.
He left his pal awaiting outside the shop's front door.
The poor thing was in agony - his tum was really sore.
'Oh, yes' the friendly chemist said, 'I have the thing for you,
Some kaolin and morphine should make him good as new.'
So three times daily from a spoon, Matthew would dose his pet,
And day by day he grew in strength. In fact the bestest yet.
At last he was recovered, and free from all his pain.
So well that he was able to go to school again.
Now dragons were not normally allowed into the school,
But as they'd never had one, they'd made a special rule.
The dragon saw the new Head and he stayed outside the gate.
'If he's just like the last one, he'll give me tummy ache!'

*J G Ryder*

## PUPPY LOVE

Cute puppies aren't all little angels,
I'm sorry it has to be said!
They pee on the floor, scratch at the door,
and leave biscuit crumbs in your bed.

You spend half your time letting them out,
the other half getting them in.
They chew up the post, shred the loo roll,
and overturn everyone's bin.

They pull up your flowers, dig holes in the lawn,
cry through the night, then wake you at dawn!
They lick clean their privates, whenever you're eating,
they sniff every bottom, it's their way of greeting.

Nine times out of ten, when posh neighbours call,
they step in a pile, he's left in the hall!
They bark at the telly, steal from the table,
bite through their leads and the video cable.

Despite all their faults in dogs you will find,
a friend who is faithful, loyal and kind.
A puppy will bring you much strife and commotion
but this can't compare with lifelong devotion.

*Nikki Barker*

# PUSSKINS

I found a cat he was smoky grey
I put him in a basket for the day.
but now it seems he is here to stay.
He chases birds, looks for mice and rats,
he does not like bees or Siamese cats.
He is very careful, does not walk on the plants
he occasionally stops to sniff at some ants.
Who hurry and scurry between crevice and stone
he has no feline friends but is never alone.
He waits for the children to come out and play
and under a bush sheltered, he is happy to stay.
Once he ventured closer and nearer
as he wanted to see the little girl clearer,
and what was happening over the fence.
His fur it bristled and his muscles were tense
a little girl was crying with pain.
She could not get up, she tried in vain
she cried for her mother, her sister, her dad.
She cried and she cried and the pain was so bad.
Pusskins knew that something was wrong
and that he must help, so mewed his loudest song.
Then he jumped on the fence, gave a bloodcurdling mew
and a stone came hurtling into view.
It hit him and hurt him, but he was full of pride
he had helped the little girl, she was carried inside.
Now the child is better, but Pusskins still bears a scar,
but he is the proudest, and best loved cat by far.

***M E C Houlden***

# DE MORTUIS

When one is getting on a bit
or like me, getting on a lot,
there's a certain satisfaction
in remembering the others who did not.
The keenest readers of the daily obits
are those who seem, to other eyes,
prime qualifiers to receive that service,
but somehow manage to survive.
And having the unquestionable advantage
of being still alive, can be quite free
to speak with smug familiarity
and patronisingly of the just now dead
in ways unthinkable when they were here.
'Poor old Frank. Pity he didn't make
the grade. He did quite well, of course.
An MBE, vice-chairman, all that sort of thing.
But - never mind! It's best I say no more.'
Which all takes place with plenty more besides
above ground level, where there's ample room
to expand into the space Frank left behind.
And leaves us wondering what, if he returned,
he would reply. Return? Not Frank!
Despite our hopes, or fears - we can rely
upon his feel for doing the right thing
and once he's dead . . . stay dead!

**Bill Johnson**

# SIGN OF THE TIMES

The world is buzzing with the noises
of communication,
But silence can be just as full
of useful information.

So let eyes take time
to appreciate
Just what silent hands
are able to relate.

A myriad of thoughts and feelings,
emotions, conjured up in sign;
A crystal clear, but silent, picture
can be instantly 'on line'.

With hands full of expression,
so much more can be conveyed
Than by using phones and faxes,
and by other means man-made.

Natural, pure communication,
information sent through 'mimes',
Without need for noises or frustration,
surely a true 'sign' of the times!

*Vikki Silverlock*

## FUTURE PETS 2000

We all must work together
animal future must be the best!
How our children love them.
The world, belongs to pets!
We must save all our pets.
Our pets will have a future
loving lambs, cows and horses.
Sweetest pets throughout our land.
We must protect all our pets.
Dogs, cats, birds and all.
This way, for future pets.
How they help us all!
They do their best, keeps us happy.
Awards and medals for our pets
memorable pets. Year 2000.
How sweet, calm, they want to live.
Please help our future pets.
Trophies, trophies, they love to win.
All give us, love and comfort!
Look at our pets, how pure!
Healthy cats, birds and dogs, 2000!
Homely pets, they love us all.
Warm, walking with our dogs,
floods galore, we love our pets.
Animals choice - Year 2000 . . .

*Dorothy Cole*

## SILENCE

What thoughts and locked experience
in your immobile frame!
Have you seen a field of buttercups?
And danced in falling rain!
Did you ride the breeze of summer?
To shades of autumn meet
with all the joys of morrow
laying at your fee.
Did age creep up unknowingly?
Did youth embrace the years?
And is the present fruitful
or trapped in bygone fears?
Who cares to know
the reason why!
You laughed, did cry,
now sleep!
Such pity priceless treasures
forever you will keep!

*J A Woodward*

# YAK! YAK! YAK!

*Joe:*

Please Flo, let's have a conversation.
You surely cannot mean to cut
off *all* communication?
You've left your new Fedora hat.

I still can feel you everywhere.
The imprint where your head has lain,
your subtle fragrance in the air.
I'm telling you - *I am in pain . . .*

How could you think to end it so
three years of love and scrimp and share -
with just this scrawl - '*I'm leaving, Flo.*'
One word for every flaming year!

We need some sessions with Relate.
They'll help us sort this latest blip.
Improve our sex life and create
a good and lasting partnership.

   I can't do all this on my own
   so *please* pick up the telephone.

*Flo:*

*Poor Joe! What can I say with tact*
*that hasn't all been said before.*
*Why can't you grasp the simple fact*
*we're not an item any more?*

*I know you want to yak, yak, yak!*
*But there's no future in the past.*
*I haven't time to ring you back*
*. . . and please don't watch the flipping post.*

*Of course I'll come and get my hat*
*but let's make sure it stays at that!*

**Ursula Kiernan**

## ON THE USE OF WORDS

With many good words we are blessed
with which to satisfy our zest
for literary or oral test -
assent or contradiction.

Yet, words offensive to the ear,
(whose meaning never was quite clear)
are often used instead, I fear,
and carry no conviction.

Our dictionaries are designed
to serve the purpose of mankind
and aid the process of the mind
when writing fact or fiction!

So many different words they give -
verb and noun and adjective, and yet
how many, while they live,
include most in their diction?

With all these words at our command,
I find it hard to understand
why I should find on every hand
such evident restriction.

The adjective, so often heard,
(a most abused and ill-used word!)
Has not a little wrath incurred,
and quite a lot of friction!

So, let us study while we may,
our dictionary, day by day,
eradicating in this way
this widely spread affliction!

*Noel Egbert Williamson*

## FORWARD IN TIME

To travel forward - what would you wish?
To fly to the future in a saucer-like dish!
To move in a thought, quick as a flash
before you'd even made a mistake
to put it right, before too late!

Wouldn't it be nice to go to a place,
without any effort, without leaving a trace.
To travel forward in time and space
maybe even win the race!

Times are changing - people are too.
The future is nearer than you think.
Right here beside you
E're you blink . . . !

*Aileen Andrews*

## THE BLITZ

My heartbeats filled my head
I held my breath. You held my hand
and waited.
The explosion came at last.
The blast . . .
Shattering the windows, but the brown sticky tape
held the glass, away from us.
Plaster fell like grey snow.
Still choking on the dust we know, we are alive.
Later on I found my friends were dead,
drowned, whilst they slept in the shelter
underground.
Our two passes stood on the shelf unused.
For we were three and there were only two.
So lady luck or God or fate,
would not let us separate.
And so the bombs on London soon would end
and we would carry on and live.

But not our friends!

*Christine Clark*

## MILLENNIUM MENU

We've put faith on hold in this new age fog!
Couch potatoes served with bytes, bits and chips.
Microwaved; digital or analogue.
Programmed; praying after we hear the pips.
We've created a life of illusion,
Priced, scanned and labelled to media cries.
Packaged hope in a web of confusion.
Thrown away love to integrate with lies.
This New Year let's re-boot/change direction,
Erase the bug from deep within our soul.
And open the file that leads to His Son.
Key in: faith, hope and love that makes us whole,
Close down: doubt, despair, apathy and hate.
Access God's heart; then we can celebrate!

*Susan M Billington*

## CALL ON GOD

Alexander Graham Bell, we owe so much to you -
The troubles you endured, and the trials you went through.
Before your phone was sold in every shop on every street
Long distance calls were still to come, so people had to meet.

People laughed, they disbelieved your phone would work or sell,
But you hung on in there - for your name did ring a Bell!
So from my heart I want to say you made the world much better -
For without your phone invention one just had to write a letter!

But now the lines are buzzing - for your scheme got off the ground.
And though it's often cheap to call, it can be dear I've found.
But God, our Heavenly Father doesn't charge - with Him it's free
And you can talk without a bill, just pray to Him and see.

So when you're feeling lost and low and need a friend to care.
Call on God - He'll answer you for He is always there.
He just longs to hear from you - He doesn't even slumber,
Talk to God at anytime by dialling up His number.

God wants that relationship; He needs communication -
And in turn He'll speak to you through every situation.
You'll know Him by His kindness and His everlasting Power;
And He'll shower His love and blessings on you hour after hour.

He is your loving Father and He's just a thought away,
And it would make Him happy if to Him you kneel and pray.
He'll never be too busy as He wants to hear from you,
About the good things in your life and all the bad things too.

He doesn't go out shopping or strike for better pay -
God is always listening - every night and every day.
No messages are taken; all prayers are heaven-directed
Pray in the name of Jesus and you will be connected.

So, God bless all the users of the phone - and may they pay
Bills reduced with off-peak cuts and discounts every day.
And speak to those who find it hard to utter up a prayer
Please touch their lives and let them know that You are always there.

*Susan Kendall*

# ONE IN A MILLION

In the flare of light
pressing back the dark,
A silver sheet of rain
patrolled back and forth.
A bubbling beef-stew terrain
thickened by the meat of God's life
taken
A man raised his metal head
above his wood-lined chamber.
To peep at truth within his mind
know the silent unknown planet.
Then metal whizzed and whined,
and he lay down to sleep
forever.

*P Butler*

## THE BRAILLE SHORTHAND MACHINE

I have no time to sit and dream,
As I work the keys of my braille machine,
Just a small machine, but a great invention,
A most useful one, too, in my contention,
For with it I can write at various speeds,
It embosses the dots for all my needs,
With six small dots in different formations,
I can write all my own communications,
And when I sit in the office for shorthand dictation,
Of letters and memos and suchlike information,
The keys on my brailler are working full-time,
And the spacebar is adding its own rhythm and rhyme,
But when work is finished at the end of the day,
And my shorthand machine is packed safely away,
Then I have time to sit and to dream,
And give thanks for the invention of the braille shorthand machine.

*Ralph C Davis*

# ESPECIALLY MO

We liked our ducks. They were bright
and friendly.
(Whereas their mindless sisters, the hens,
were scatty.)
Eeeny, Meeny, Miny and Mo had character.
They would quack their way
to the back door, punctually,
with purpose and determination,
demanding food.
Our ducks were sensible, organised;
they knew what life is about
and pursued it, muddily.
Mo became afflicted with a bad foot
a  nd l  imp  ed.
My mother bathed the bad foot
in hot water
every four hours,
right round the clock,
sympathetically.

Mo was grateful
and loved her faithfully.
We children said: 'Mummy loves Mo
as much as us
(even more?)'
Which was unfair. She loved us.
My advice is:
If you want company, fun, challenge, response,
as well as eggs.
Then, have ducks.

*Katharine Holmstrom*

## PAWS FOR THOUGHT

My pampered puss was once a stray
who just walked in and chose to stay.
We'd sit here alone just Tibby and me
a friendly old moggy he used to be.
He would sit on my lap, purring away
always with me night and day.
His coat was black and shiny
and eyes of palest green.
Quite a handsome feline
of character supreme.

He lifted his paw when wanting to be fed
then slept it off all day on the bed.
He fought everything that came too near
and once came in with a cauliflower ear.
Sometimes he was naughty
and jumped on the table.
Or knocked over a vase
and swung on a cable.
When my son brought home a prize fish
Tibby decided to devour the dish.

One day he became poorly
and passed away.
We were all upset that sad day.
Goodbye little friend, we had to part
You dear old moggy - who stole my heart.

*Lilian France*

## LAZY BONES

Butch is large and black
a lazy Labrador in fact.
We love him dearly
yet to exercise him is a chore.
He will walk a little
take a short-sharp run.
But mostly prefers to lie in the sun.

He can catch anything first time
that is, if he wants to - fine!
But when not to his liking
he ignores the morsel completely
and becomes suddenly extremely sleepy.
Even at the call of dinner-time
lacks the energy to wine and dine.

The fireside in winter is his favourite place
and makes for it in indecent haste.
He will lie there for hours on end
no-one can get near,
as he takes up so much room.
Perhaps he knows a thing or two
why waste energy, if it's just not you!

***Diane York***

## THE CONFESSIONS OF HENRY

I am a gangster cat you may be sure
I live in Liverpool and life's no bore.
I'm boss of all the cats
I'm good at catching rats
I'm fond of little pats . . . and purr for more!

I have my own HQ in an old house.
The entrance fee (to friends) is one dead mouse.
I'm top cat of the street
I walk on velvet feet
I love to eat fresh meat . . . and sometimes Scouse!

My proper name is Henry . . . be it known
but the neighbours all know me as Al Capone.
I'm black from head to foot
just like a piece of soot.
I love to walk, and fight, and hunt . . . alone.

Yes! I am a gangster cat you see
the other Toms and Queens defer to me.
I know I am the best . . .
Not quite like the rest
So kneel and pay your homage just to me!

*Clare Snead*

## SHEPHERD'S DELIGHT

Forget the myth of Miss Bo-Peep
Good shepherds do not lose their sheep!
Why this rapport should be so good
they're just like friends, they're understood.
No sheepish words that they can say
but actions give their minds away.
A forlorn look, no appetite
are warning signs that all's not right.
An ailing sheep it must be said
without due care, will soon be dead.
Parted from the flock we see
that giving birth needs privacy.
Well away from prying eyes
upon the ground, prostrate he lies.
A single lamb - but that is fair
because last year, she dropped a pair.
To be licked dry is all it takes
to forge a bond that nothing breaks.
Then tottering on unsteady feet
instinct guides to mother's teat.
Of warm colostrum takes his fill.
he's now immune to any chill.
Satisfied he shakes his back,
tomorrow, gambols with the pack.
Born with breeding pedigree
He is lucky, he's a he.
He could have faced a dire fate
all mint flavoured on a plate.
Forget mutton dressed as lamb
He's an Aries - he's a ram . . .

*J T Fall*

# WUFFIE'S LOVE

The day that Wuffie came to stay was a day of joy and laughter
The big sad eyes, the loppy grin, the paws all gangling after
Ben, wherever Ben might go,
And Ben took Wuffie to his heart, and Wuffie loved Ben so.
'Now Wuffie, you must learn to sit, to give a paw, to stay.'
But Wuffie thought it so much fun - another game to play!
He'd scamper off around and round, while trying to catch his tail.
'You're supposed to stay!' cried fed up Ben, but Wuff was in
full sail!
'You're supposed to sit!' shrieked Ben to him, but Wuff
just gave a loppy grin.

The days seemed long and warm and gold, with endless hours of fun,
And neither saw the years grow old, Wuff kept them ever young.
If Ben was sad, then so was Wuff, his head upon Ben's knee.
Big sad eyes as if to say ''S okay, you've still got me.'
Inseparable, the two friends were as Ben was growing up,
And Wuffie never felt his years, still silly as a pup.
But came the day, the twelfth of May, when Wuffie played no more,
Ben called to him, of the loppy grin, but he couldn't make the door.
'I can't go on,' the old eyes said, and Ben held Wuffie tight
As Wuffie sighed, and Ben just cried.
So far into the night.

Death could not break the bond of love, that Wuffie shared with Ben,
He'd oft return to run a new, o'er field and moor and fen.
Or curl up with Ben asleep, all paws and arms entwined,
Just as they had throughout the years, in sleep, Ben's grief was kind.
Ben didn't really know he came - though sometimes he'd just feel
His best friend there, still by his side, still running at his heel.
And so with Ben old Wuff would run, they were never far apart,
And Wuffie loved Ben, all Ben's life
And life-long, filled Ben's heart.

*Alison Forbes*

## STRAY

Our lives were standing water
until you came, sweet ginger flame,
and marmite coloured pawprints, on surfaces
once milky clean, your signature,
young puss without a name.

Our home is neatened and fitted,
(though the bird-table may be untidy).
Plastic mainly, plus loyalty cards.
In Legoland, in a secular age,
we cannot fall from grace.
But you came, disorganised us, orange flame
though a god you must not be, erratic cat
We'll call you darling Furface.

*Jennifer McDonald*

# THE PHONE

What would it be like without a phone?
We couldn't ever contact a friend from home.
We would sit and be miserable and all alone,
with nothing to do but moan and groan.
We are so lucky today when bored
to be able to phone someone abroad.
Yes, the phone is the best thing yet
to be able to pick up and ring in a bet.

***D N Snow***

# IN THE SKY

The distant drone becomes closer, then it recedes and returns, a sound
Which is heard in ever decreasing circles until now overhead.
A stationary helicopter's powerful beam sweeps the ground.
Get away thieves caught on camera, pursued by a police car as
                                                    they fled.

An urgent call to a roof-top scene before returning to their base.
Someone's depression has never been blacker, snapped mind,
                                            no hope in sight.
On extended ladders Fire Officers calmly talk watching his face.
Distracted by the sudden noise the fire-crew grab him,
                                            there is no fight.

Most accident victims can be airlifted, those on a motorway
With a speed which an ambulance may not match through solid
                                            traffic queues.
New technology has proved to be an asset in this modern day
Whether the cost justifies the means, depend on people's
                                            varied views.

*Mary E Beale*

# TELECOMMUNICATIONS

The best invention is the telephone
especially if you have to live alone.
When you have a problem in the night
you can inform someone of your plight.
Sometimes there's good news at your end
things that you must pass on to a friend.
There are annoyances being rung by Double Glazing
the times they call are quite amazing.
We all love to hear of pregnant joy
and say 'Well tell me which? A girl or boy?'
Practically anywhere in the world, your voice can go
getting you answers to the questions you want to know.
Of course there are times when news is sad
on the whole, most conversations make you glad.
That you have had a telephone installed
particularly when someone you love has called.
Very expensive, but so worthwhile.
I cannot wait to get my own mobile!

*Edna M Whiter*

# SAMMY

You are a lovely golden cat.
Your coat so soft and clean.
Your eyes like two bright saucers
When at night they gleam.

You purr and play until it's time
for you to have your fish.
You follow me around and play
until you get your wish.

But when it's put in front of you,
one sniff and off you pad.
For to catch a mouse or two
for you're a clever lad.

Although I'm sure the mouse you'd like
for me to cook instead.
You would only poke it with your paw
then off you'd go to bed.

***Beryl Smyter***

## COCK PHEASANT

Gorgeous with red comb, green neck, sweeping tail,
You strut, perhaps not proud but set to win
Your chosen mate affecting carelessness.
Some see in you a dinner, some a challenge
To marksmanship. But you are welcome here,
A guest and an adornment to my garden.

*Angus Sinclair*

## PRISONERS

Hear the clank of heavy chain
and the trudge of dead men's feet;
Prisoners walk again.
Mortals robbed of self-esteem
to an early grave must go.
Why must this be so?
Wasted lives full of despair
ebb out in utter fruitlessness.
'Freedom!' they cry.
For why?
To seek out, murder and destroy.
All is vanity.
Where are the threads of decency
that cradle the innocent?
Savour the sweet essence of humanity;
It too is passing.
Listen! You can hear
the loud clank of looped chain;
Prisoners freed to walk again.

*Heather Henning*

# ARTHUR

Arthur is getting old, he is more than fourteen years.
There are times he's been a rascal, had me close to tears.
I can recall quite vividly, when he was a pup,
we had decorated, put new wallpaper up.
I went out for a little while, just to the local store,
on my return the wallpaper was strewn around the floor.
When he is scared or lonely he'll chew anything he can.
He has chewed door-frames and cushions, the seat of my son's van.
He is happy when we have visitors, with people he is good.
With other dogs he is the tops, and he makes that understood.
He's a Staffordshire bull terrier - with him dogs do not tamper
they bark at him but when he growls, they stop and off they scamper.
If neighbours leave their doors open, he will always risk it,
he'll get in, and won't come out till they give him a biscuit.
When he wants to go walkies, he lets us know what it's about.
He opens wide his mouth, and the sound that he makes is *out!*

*Elizabeth Wren*

## BUT NOT LAST LOVE

My cat would show in many ways
his perfect Love to start our days -
with patting back, loud purr and look,
or washing hair to wake me up.

When left in house, there'd often be
a window-watch to welcome me;
but, if too long, then he'd repair
to wait and sleep upon my chair.

If so asleep, the key in door
would see him mewing there before
I'd entered; then his rubbing ploy
on furniture revealed his joy.

In car: left out, he'd never roam
but fly to greet me safely home,
skip-prance at feet from garage track,
and only eat when I was back.

At gardening, he'd trail me round;
on Loving talk he'd roll the ground.
Yards' start; I'd lose each lawn/home race;
but hedge-top walk reduced his pace.

Play-pats on head from almond tree
and finger/paw fights pleasured me.
Love-biting hand, long gaze to eyes,
keen psychic sense: Remembrance sighs.

To his own bed I bore him for
a snuffle-wash (and later snore!)
then 'Goodnight' paw-to-finger pat
would end day's Love from 'tiger' cat.

Came 'Goodbye' final finger-pat;
This World's last Love from Tick, my cat.

**_Tony Hughes-Southwart_**

## THE MONSTER

Vicki's monster was a huge creature.
A creature that was always there,
putting her in fear.
It had razor sharp teeth
breathing fire as was its bequeath.

Although this Titan was not the chief,
it knew how to do its party piece.
Making it liked the least,
for this was truly an awful beast.
That caused everyone grief,
so there was never any peace.
Therefore unhappiness increased
and in short, it never ceased.

Its roar rose like yeast.
Vicki thought when would she be released,
let off its evil leash.
Where exactly it came from was not clear.
And to ask it, who would dare?
As it stares with five terrifying eyes.

Vicki hopes and prays that it would go away
but it looks like it is here to stay.
This was something Vicki could not bare,
even monsters died somewhere.
She told herself trying to relax.

'*Victoria Green!*
You're not paying attention it would seem!'
Victoria's monster had spoken.
Mr Dean her science teacher,
who was always so mean.
Waking her up from her unruly day-dream.

*Ali Sebastian*

# MY MATE MAX

Max has a special place in my heart,
with his deep, warm and friendly bark.
He knows when life is rough or sad,
and knows just when I'm feeling glad.

With coat of shining glossy hue,
when he's around I can't be blue.
He has his moments when he's deaf,
and does not appreciate being left.

He's jealous when I'm on the phone
but will willingly share with me his bone.
A gentle giant with love to give,
perhaps not now so long to live.

Old age, like ivy gently creeps
now, far more he rests and sleeps.
But still his welcome knows no bounds,
My mate Max, one of God's special hounds.

*Lyn Errington*

## THE MAIDEN VOYAGE

Serene and tranquil the ocean,
People getting ready to sail,
Shouts of Bon Voyage,
Silhouettes waving from the rail.

Gliding effortlessly out beyond,
A magnificent giant of steel,
Navigating the lanes of the sea,
The proud captain at the wheel.

Majestic, the ship sailed on,
Merriment pervaded the air,
Champagne corks exploding,
Un-noticed an iceberg was near.

Thick fog had also descended,
The competent captain kept calm,
This was her maiden voyage,
His ship would come to no harm.

Indestructible they had said,
The finest they had ever built,
A mighty jolt, engines failed,
The Titanic started to tilt.

Screams of fear from the dying,
Amidst cries of horror and fright.
A hymn was sung on the deck,
As the Titanic sunk that night.

The souls of the dead drifted on,
The tormented wreck, once their host,
Journeyed down to the bottom of the sea,
The harbour of shipyard ghosts.

*Glennis Norne*

## BEWILDERMENT

I have a new Font Writer
It only came today
So excuse the many errors
That will surely come my way.

What's 'formatting' and 'dialogue',
'Spreadsheets' and 'cursors' too?
And 'menus' do not list good food
And what must I 'undo'?

Why should I change my typeface
From 'Dutch', to 'Script', to 'Swiss'?
Some day I'll understand it all
And life will be pure bliss!

'Attach merge file', 'Press P to print'
This very silly ode.
'Access the spreadsheets', 'Block the cells'.
Why can't I crack this code?

Perhaps I should go back in time
To my John Bull stamp and pad
It surely would be slower
But it might not drive me mad!

*Eileen M Pratt*

## Kosovo, a Human Tragedy

As I move about my garden
in sunshine or in shade,
the thought is there
on the fringes of my mind,
and the horror cannot be laid
down like gardening tools
and put away.

As I move about my garden
I'm troubled in my mind,
there's ethnic cleansing going on
in a once forgotten land,
and the digging of mass graves
for the villages in flames
and the families on fire.

The thought is in my mind
in this haven of my peace,
of refugees in grievous tears
for the loved ones killed
at random and homes
and land they cherished,
they may never see again.

The thought is in my mind
and somewhat mixed with shame,
that the west can do so little
for the families in flames
but make a resolution,
more than a little late,
that tyrants *will* be punished,
and justice *can* prevail.

**Monica Redhead**

## WRITING OFF THE WALL

Are you a scholar, how much do you read?

> I read what I hear.

How much do you hear?

> Through great silences
> the utterances of the absent
> to the unborn
> are resurrected.

How much do you see?

> Through long light
> the windows of the eyes
> catching in the dust the words
> displayed like butterflies
> humans fixed
> in a tunnel of time
> the echo
> up to date peace
> between past and present.

How much do you remember?

> Shapes
> of stillness implanting forgetfulness
> within themselves

What is their truth?

> Truth is flexible
> nothing could be older
> 'til he quietly passes
> into oblivion
> dying peacefully
> but not the writing on the wall.

*A Thompson*

## THE INTERLOPER

He came to us on a hot summer's day,
We were lazing away the afternoon
in the summer house.
Glasses of ice cold lemonade
and chilled bowls of strawberries beside us,
Robert and I were content.

Then in he strolled, long legged,
Sleek as an otter, the colour of spun gold.
He walked in, looked straight at us both,
Flicked his tail
And slowly lay down in the sunshine.

We never spoke about his coming,
One glance at each other was enough
To know the rightness of him being there,
We never found out where he came from,
We never cared.

We named him Amber,
He has been with us now for eight years.
His favourite place is still the summer house
And his love is eternal.

*Dorothy M Kemp*

# HUNTER ON THE HEARTH RUG

Beauteous beast who lies before the fire,
Silken paw out-stretched and softly curled,
Sleek head rests against the rug in soft repose,
No hint now of latent power when, flashing claws unfurled,
Ears pricked forward, whiskers trembling with desire,
The savage hunter stalks his prey,
With twitching tail and golden orbs of eyes, now closed,
Fixed firmly on a luckless bird or mouse,
His movements sinuous and swift, his senses keen,
They try in vain to dodge that final pounce,
That leaves them victim to those sharp white teeth
Which now are hid by sleeping lips of velvet fur.
He stirs and wakes, gently licks a paw with pink-tipped tongue,
Deft and dainty movements, while from his throat a purr
Rumbles forth to show contentment with his world.
The golden eyes are slants of pleasure, glancing up at me,
He condescends to rise with languid movements,
Pausing first to stretch, he leaps upon my knee,
Rubs his face against me curling round about,
The purr grows louder as I stroke his soft, warm fur,
So cuddly now and yet, the fleeting glimpse of claws stretched out
Before he leapt reminds me that the pet I hold by day,
Loveable and lordly, owning, never owned,
By night, as nature made him, a snarling beast of prey,
The hearth rug is his pleasure, but his hunting ground his home.

*Ailsa Keen*

## CSAR

Often known as 'Bear',
I'm big and strong,
with four huge paws,
and I'm very long
from the tip of my tail
to my long white nose,
which burrows in the deepest snows.
I've deep, dark eyes
and a thick white coat,
do I come from some place quite remote?
With months of darkness, frozen plains,
Polar ice caps, freezing rains?
Yes! Scottish Borders are my home,
and forest walks I love to roam,
Deep Syke and Cloiche and Ladyurd
and though it almost seems absurd
I never really feel that cold
my humans do, as they get old.
West Linton village is my base
from where I walk most every place,
To Tocherknowe and Baddingsgill,
Wakefield, Lynedale, Mendick Hill.
Then home to rest and build up strength.
It seems they'll go to any length,
to tire me out, with sticks and rings
to make me run, retrieving things,
but in the end it's they who flag,
exhausted like an empty bag,
while I'm still willing to go far,
their German Shepherd dog, I'm 'Csar'.

*Neil Patterson*

## OSCAR

Two big brown eyes are shining, a coat of silver and gold
You brought us so much happiness, and you're only three years old
We bless the day we bought you, a bundle of darkest fur
No larger than a kitten, and mischief everywhere

You chewed our shoes and furniture, until it made you sick
And when we scolded you, you gave our hand a lick
You know when we are angry, and you have made us cross
You cock your head, and seem to say 'Well Mother is the boss'

We give you the name of 'Oscar' what a name for a Yorkie
Thought we
But an event that happened recently, fit him to a tee
One day I left the door ajar, and in the lounge I sat
An intruder entered my kitchen, Oscar didn't stand for that

Head alert, ears upright, to investigate he went
Growling, baring fangs with intent
And as I went to see, what the noise was all about
So astonished was I, I couldn't even shout

He held the man against the wall, he wouldn't let him move
So terrified was the man, his innocence he tried to prove
I only wanted a fiver changed, his excuse was so slim
Then thinking I slammed the door on him
Oscar barked and kept guard, he wouldn't budge at all
So I left him there, tied the door, and gave the police a call
At last the police arrived, took the man away
Oscar watched, and wagged his tail, the hero of the day.

*Mary Seddon*

## THE ELEPHANT

The elephant is super strong, a giant in the animal world.
He trumpets so loud when he tramps along. With his trunk so
neatly furled.
I've often longed for a ride on his back, though a mountain
I'd rather climb.
I'd carry a Mac in a haversack, and a clock
To tick and chime.

What fun it would be when that elephant free,
Would uncurl his flexible trunk,
It just goes to show with much water in flow,
The gallons he's sucked up or drunk.

At the foot of the palm he reaches with charm,
Bananas in huge yellow bunches.
Just fancy the scene where Jumbo has been,
Eating dinner, fresh snacks, and quick lunches.

He's kind to the old folk, white mice and the blind.
For good deeds he never forgets.
He's not one to bungle a walk in the jungle,
In the land where the sun never sets!

*Geoffrey N Nuttall*

## HODDY'S ODE

Seven last Sunday.
(Not supposed to live till five.)
Born with a poorly heart, too long a nose,
And other things beside.

So many pills at mealtimes,
So many visits to the vet.
My heart is bad when it is hot,
My legs so stiff when it is wet.

But I am such a lucky dog.
I've had a lovely life.
My 'human mums' protect me
From too much stress and strife.

Holidays on Dartmoor,
Picnics on the beach.
My family all around me
Always within my reach.

Four cats to keep me company.
A bed for sleep at night.
And if I wake from troubled dreams
Someone to hold me tight.

I love them all so very much
I know that they love me.
I do my very doggy best
I know they'd all agree.

I kiss them and I wag my tail
I'm good as good can be!
I am their 'darling Cavalier',
And they're 'my family'.

*Ann Linney*

## THE PIPE

The pipe he found was bubble
A veritable treasure
For me it spelt trouble
For him it meant pleasure
Found in the fields
With a lifetime of grime
His archaeological find
In a bucket that week
To clean out the world
He patiently waited
To give it a whirl
At last with eyes sparkling
Cold nose checked it out
My canine comedian
The happiest out.

*Anne Codling*

# FOUR-LEGGED FRIENDS

They say two is company and three is a crowd
But Meg doesn't think so barking out loud

Felix the cat is now taking the lead
With dainty paw poised she will wait and succeed

So cleverly still she knows how to frustrate
Puppy Meg's play and then it's too late!

A swift slender paw brings a tease and a fright
And then we meet James who is grey brown and white

Hopping and nibbling content in his run
Meg runs to annoy and he joins in the fun

The fence is no object as wet noses meet
And James on his hind legs looks rather neat!

A friendly game starts as they chase alongside
But Meg gets impatient when James runs to hide

Barking and digging the earth in a hurry
Meg paws through the fence but James has no worry!

Felix now gently leaps onto the run
Prowling to settle and preen in the sun

They say two is company and three is a crowd
Meg still doesn't think so barking out loud!

*Rebecca Punter*

## CHRONICLES OF THE 20TH CENTURY

The 20th Century witnessed Europe's darkest history
A case in point was the Holocaust
Marked as the worst barbarous creature was mankind
About 50 millions were killed by 1945
Across Europe in bombed-out cities and towns
Refugees were trying to get to their homes
Rebuilding their shattered lives was the hope of millions
From the trauma of rape
At the hands of invading armies
Women and girls by the thousands
Were trying to recover
While grieving for their lost husbands and parents
With the second half of the 20th Century
Came the collapse of Colonialism and the fall of Communism

Wars continued even by the end of World War II
About 160 of these around the globe waged
Caused 7 million battlefield deaths and 30 million civilian deaths
Now in the '90s lethal conflicts fired by burning hatred
Killed not only soldiers but also thousands of civilians
With the proliferation of modern weapons
Children soldiers are now part of the human follies

In mostly poorest countries they are operating
Even wire-guided missiles used in modern wars
Often reach not the targets for which they are designed
As Desert Fox operations recently proved
A wilderness of misery and ruin was usually provoked

Will the genocide and bombing raid in Kosovo
signal the end of that ugly and sickening picture
With the collapse of religious values
Has emerged a flood of moral degradation
The 20th Century has also gone through.

*Dan Chellumben*

## SURF THE NET?

Surf the net I hear them say, but will I get my feet wet?
But my little mouse knows his way around so I won't fuss and fret

This computer's not like my old typewriter, it's got a life of its own
It speaks to me, it beeps and burps, but can it answer my phone?

This E mail lark is all the rage my mailbox is often full
At least they're not all circulars and my dog can't chew them all

And all this talk of webs and nets just leaves me full of dread
I think I need an idiot's guide to help me get ahead

I have a little helper though, who sits upon the screen
He taps upon the VDU so he's heard as well as seen

He's an animated paper clip that winks and jigs around
And if I'm stuck for answers he comes up trumps I've found

Now with this IT package I can do things my own way
With faxes I can do my job by staying home all day!

My banking I can do on line, keeping finances in the black
I can even check my stocks and shares, all I need is just the knack

So never mind the mobile phones, put your pens away for good
And we'll all correspond the modern way, if only that we could.

*Jean Selmes*

## COMMUNICATION AND HOOVERING

Writing takes up your hoovering time,
Or hoovering takes up your writing time.

Whichever way you want to see it,
I've just written this,
So I can't have been hoovering.

Oscar Wilde never said this.

Some people write *and* hoover,

. . . At the risk of burning themselves out.

**Steve Taylor**

## MUGS DAIGNEAULT

Where flows the muddy Don its languid way
And tram cars ply the urban trail;
Stands a refuge there, where the cast-offs may
Find undue demise or the 'Holy Grail'.
Came a kindly pair with a worthwhile sheen;
And their bearing spoke to the reason why
His prospects soared with their chatter keen
For the honeyskin pup with the searching eye.
'Walk no further down this long doleful line;
Wrench your hearts no more though they worthy be;
I'm the one you seek and I'll fit in fine;
Mutts aplenty here but they can't match me.'
A clown, a prince, a comfort zone;
In character no weakness found;
A demon when a ball is thrown;
A poster for your local pound.
Ever mindful how we feel, dog of velvet and of steel.

*William Ailbe O'Neill*

# MY PALS

I'm writing about my two canines
they are friends in every way,
black and white Border collies
loved and fed every day.

Long walks I leave to my husband
five miles is nothing to him,
he's out for more than three hours
at least it keeps him quite trim.

The postman is really quite popular
it really makes their day,
they wait near the door for hours
to grab letters and then run away.

We take them away on holiday
in our caravan they're good as can be,
as soon as we start all our packing
they are howling and barking with glee.

Trips to the vet is so awful
a nightmare is all I can say,
two very frightened doggies
and wee on the floor, by the way.

But I would be lost without them
they are faithful and ever so true,
you can never pay what their life's worth
and extreme love they give just to you.

**_Janet Hall_**

## PETS AND VETS

I took our dog Patch,
He's our family pet,
A mild mannered, tail wagging pooch,
Along to see the vet,

After some waiting around,
I read an article on rabies,
Patch had barely raised an eyelid,
At the cockatoo, kittens and a terrapin and her babies,

But once on the vet's table,
For his examination, his once over,
He turned into a snarling snapping,
Aggressive angry nasty little rover,

The vet was taken aback,
I was embarrassed to say the least,
Because my lovely little dog,
Was transformed into a savage beast,

The vet was bitten twice,
Blood dripped onto the floor,
Then Patch chased the vet,
Who fled through the surgery door,

Then the vet returned both calm and collected,
Minus his white coat,
which was blood-stained and ripped,
He took a deep breath and nervously cleared his throat,

Patch led on the table,
Contained and rather non-plussed,
The vet carried out his examination,
Patch offered no resistance, in fact he wasn't even fussed,

So as for men in white coats, Patch takes an instant dislike,
Gladly he will chase them all off into the night.

*P J Littlefield*

# BRUCE

I walked with him, in all kinds of weather,
We were seldom apart, always together.
He's in my thoughts, when I'm alone,
It's been so long, since he had gone.
He guarded me, and, stayed by my side.
My thoughts for him, I'll never hide.
I stayed with him, right till the end.
He'll always be my faithful friend.
A man's best friend, is his dog,
These words are very true.
They'll protect you, night and day,
They'll always be there for you.
They're company, when you're lonely,
They'll also guard your home.
When you have a loving faithful friend,
You'll never be on your own.

***Catherine Fleming***

# THE LOST PRINCESS

*(Diana, Princess of Wales, died in a road accident, aged 36,*
*August 31st 1997)*

Tragic and lonesome, lovely doomed princess,
Could not some knight his banner have unfurled
To cherish and protect you in distress,
And guard you from the jackals of this world?

Of all knights-errant true you were the sum
Who won more hearts than ever armed men will,
Who sought the children, bade the orphans come,
Touched maimed and dying, the ostracised, the ill.

But you yourself were vulnerable, ensnared
By your high title, all the world endorsed;
Using your wealth to show the world you cared:
Mother of Royals, from royalty divorced.

In need of love, you had so much to give:
Diana, dead, now in our hearts you live!

***Bernard Brown***

## CAT LOVER

She slinks along the tall stone garden wall,
Like a slender model on the catwalk,
Showing off her stylish spring collection,
In the sunshine to perfection.

Seduced by the sensual swaying of her hips,
Towards a place where darkest shadows meet,
I come across her, prone on velvet green,
Using her tongue, alone, unseen.

Stroking herself meticulously, undisturbed,
Till suddenly she starts, and lifts her head.
Sensing something breathing, something there,
She springs like a tiger through the air.

Her raging claws rip into tender flesh.
Seized lie a tiny, darting, hapless mouse,
I struggle to survive; but still my heart
Is played with first, then torn apart.

I'm feverish, in bed alone at night.
Pale moonlight falls across the crumpled sheets.
I can see at the window, from where I lie,
Her silhouette against the sky.

What game is this? She left me long ago.
There's nothing, no one, on the garden wall;
But the mind, knowing well she once was there,
Plays cat and mouse with vacant air.

She slinks along the tall stone garden wall,
Like a slender model on the catwalk,
Free from the sadness of recollection,
Basking in her own reflection.

*AKS Shaw*

## BEN THE STRAY

On a cold, and frosty winter morn,
A sad, and lonely face forlorn.
Looks up at me as much to say,
Please take me in, it's cold today.
The scruffy bundle was invited in,
The state of him, it was a sin.
He was not fit for beast nor men,
He had no name we called him Ben.
Down at the vet's, he did object,
To make him better was a good prospect.
After some pills, a trim, and shampoo.
He soon looked as good as new.
Now that Ben is growing old
He doesn't wander from the fold.
He doesn't play much anymore
His old bones are getting sore.
We will take good care of him till the end.
On all of us he can depend.

*Katherine Summers*

## SOLDIERS

Two bodies stiffen -
Ashes again,
A second lieutenant
And one of his men

If you asked of them both
For what they had died,
The first would consider
Before he replied

He'd think over the question,
And when he had done
Say 'The answer to that
Is a difficult one'

Without hesitation
If he only could speak,
The second would mutter
'Seven shillings a week.'

*Elisabeth Ware*

# HILLSBOROUGH 1989

'Can't wait for the match' I bet a lot of people thought,
Liverpool Vs Forest, they weren't the ones that fought.
Fans turning up for the match of the year,
Not knowing what's ahead of them or trace of fear.
Flags are waving, people all excited,
All colours, creeds and kinds are once reunited.
Pressures building up on the outside as well as in,
People want to see the match and who will win.
Police are getting worried so they open up the gate,
They should have opened up the other two, but it was too late.
They start to push harder like sardines in a can,
'What about my daughters' cried out a worried man.
A policeman shrugged his shoulders, he couldn't really care,
The poor man was crying, it really wasn't fair.
People getting crushed against the tall thin railing,
Police standing still when lives they should have been saving.
The match is called off and people are on the ground,
Football posts are dragged down and bodies all around.
Families and friends looking for their mates,
Except they are lying dead and have finally met their fates.
Ambulances can't get on the pitch at all,
Dead bodies getting pushed up against the cold, hard wall.
And what is left but people traumatised,
People left alone with their lives capsized.
Even young policemen were disturbed by what they saw,
So much, they had to see doctors, it was worse than any war.
Ninety-five people died on this tragic day,
Flowers were sent and for their crime, the police had to pay.
Some families compensated, others were not,
And it is this horrific tragedy that will never be forgot.

*Kerry Hayley  (17)*

## BLACK CAT
*(Dedicated to Lady Luck)*

The sun shines warmly.
My cat sleeps cosily.
Hours pass smoothly,
Stretching out luxuriously.
Ears twitching dreamily
She yawns pink and fishily
Then licks a paw silkily.
Arranging herself deliciously
She subsides again thankfully
Sighing long and creamily,
But never, ever, guiltily.

***Elizabeth Meredith***

## NAMES?

Naming a dog is a difficult thing
And, if you don't watch, a headache will bring.
When he hears what I say,
He will wander away
Which is a bad thing
When you're trying to bring
An illustrious name
Which might bring him fame!
First, there's ordinary names like Blackie and Jo,
Minnie and Sheba and Bouncy and Bo.
There are names we give children
Like Andrew and Jim
Which are so refined that they don't suit him.
There are names that are dignified and pedigreed
Such as Sophocles, Nero and Caesar, agreed?
There are names so amusing
That most aren't enthusing
Such as Onka, Paringa and Great Jackdaw.
No wonder the doggie holds up his paw!
But, remember that dogs are aware of their name
And dislike the ones that don't bring them fame;
So, if you call Scrutable he will not come
And bounds far away, for he is *not* dumb.

*Nola B Small*

## I REMEMBER D DAY

On that great day of June the sixth, in nineteen forty-four,
I rose before the break of dawn, felt drawn towards the shore.
I felt excitement in the air, the mist had eerie feel,
As if it was the dawn of time, I felt an urge to kneel.

I knelt and prayed for freedom, an end to this long war,
Then when I raised my eyes aloft, a miracle I saw.
Through swirling mists like angels' wings, as far as I could see,
Were rows and rows of Allied ships, all heading straight for me.

I raced inland to spread the news, they're coming, it's today,
The Allied troops will land at dawn, our freedom's on its way.
Wave after wave they poured ashore, Passed by to fight inland,
Though many fell and gave their lives, lay dead on foreign sand.

So many years have now gone by, since that immortal day,
When in the mist of that June morn, I knelt alone to pray.
To all who fought upon that day, we owe our freedom now,
The future will remember them, in freedom this we vow.

So few of them still live today, so many died that year,
Died fighting for our freedom now, a freedom they'd not share.
If on that day you were not born, or were too young to go,
However can you realise, however can you know.

How felt each man to be a part, of that Armada brave,
Each laying his life on the line, a foreign soil to save.
Each never knowing if his time, to part this life was nigh,
Whilst all around him pain and death, whilst shells and bullets fly.

Show to all of those brave men, they suffered not in vain,
Just guard and cherish freedom still, ensure it will remain.
The way you live and work and play, may not be to their plan,
But for your right to make the choice, they risked all to a man.

Yet though so many fought and died, to stem dictators' might,
Your freedom's only fleeting still, it is not yours of right.
So you now hold the future years, through them you're here today,
It's in your hands so guard it well, or lose it as you may.

If ever you by carelessness, let it slip out of sight,
It's you the price will have to pay, you then who'll have to fight.
So be forever vigilant, no more such price to pay,
Let our history forever, record just one D Day.

*Alan Terry*

## ODE TO 'MITTENS'

You brought me love
Now you bring me pain
There's a void in my heart
'Cos you're gone.
A tiny morsel when we found you
As you cowered in the rain
Abandoned and alone
Now you've gone.
I warmed you and I fed you
Cleaned your matted fur
Let you snuggle on the sofa
Now you've gone.
I didn't want to keep you
The road being as it was
They drive too fast you see
So sad you're gone.
As time passed
I grew to love you
I just had to let you stay
You grew into such a beauty
On my lap you'd always lay.
You never quite 'meowed'
Just this cutest little squeak
With a wonderful bushy tail
Like a fox you were so sleek.
Eight months was such a short life
For my darling little Mittens
I'll never forget you
My special little kitten.

*Angela Watson*

# INFORMATION

We hope you have enjoyed reading this book - and that you will continue to enjoy it in the coming years.

If you like reading and writing poetry drop us a line, or give us a call, and we'll send you a free information pack.

Write to :-

**Triumph House Information
Remus House
Coltsfoot Drive
Woodston
Peterborough
PE2 9JX
(01733) 898102**